Spice Blending
to Your Own Taste

By

Ann L. Koretz

Annie's House Publishing

INTRODUCTION

A brief history about spices -

Spices used to be used traded like money. They were also used as medicine - and they still are. One that comes to mind is turmeric which is good for migraines. There is a list near the back of this book with more spice remedies. Also in this book you will find recipes for spice blends and how to use them, and some meal recipes to use the spice blends in. There is also a list of spice substitutions.

Where do you buy spices and herbs? Most commonly at the grocery store, but there you will be paying more for the packaging. They come in a variety of containers - bottles, jars, plastic bags, tins and in bulk. You can purchase spices in bulk on line, at farmers' markets or at ethnic stores.

This book talks about spice blends, dip mixes, meat rubs and dukkahs. Do you know what a dukkah is? A Dukkah is an Egyptian condiment made from spices, nuts, seeds and herbs ground together. In Egypt it is eaten with olive oil and bread (dip a crusty bread in the olive oil then into the dukkah). Use a dukkah like a cheese ball - just cover cream cheese with the dukkah then spread it on crackers or bread. It can even be sprinkled over soups and other foods.

Have you heard of **Chinese Five Spice**? It is a traditional blend, named *not* after the number of ingredients but for the five spice flavors (sour, savory, hot, sweet, pungent). The combination of these flavors is thought to create balance.

Here are some popular **spice blends** you can buy in a grocery store -

Season salt ~ Italian seasoning ~ Taco seasoning ~ Poultry seasoning ~ Chili Powder ~ Onion soup mix ~ Cinnamon Sugar ~ Onion salt ~ Pumpkin pie spice ~ Lemon pepper ~ Curry powder (you might have thought curry was a spice itself. But it's not, it's a blend).

Why make your own spice blends?

Here are a few reasons to make your own spice blends:

- You can make blends that you can't find in local stores.
- You can get different flavors for your cooking.
- You can put them together with your own taste - if you like more cinnamon and less cloves, spicy or not.
- You'll know what you're getting. No added salt, MSG or preservatives.
- Of course, you'll save money.

Your own signature spice blend makes a great gift for friends & relatives. What better hostess gift than a beautiful jar of *your* handmade special spice blend or dip mix?

Put your signature spice blend in a variety of containers.   You can even dress them up with fancy labels or ribbon to use as gifts. *NOTE - Mulling spices make a nice gift for the holidays.

Saving Money -

I bought season salt at a home party for $10.00. Then I made my own for under $2.00.

I bought Beetroot Dip mix for $15.95. Then I made my own for $5.75.

I bought Tomato & Herb Dip mix for $15.95. Then I made my own for $5.93.
                    . . . and I like mine better!

What is a "spice"?

A spice is something that flavors food. All spices are organic - meaning from a living plant. All spices are dried. Spices are usually the bark, pods, root, stalk or seed of a plant.

Nowadays all parts of fruit & veggies (beets, garlic, onions), when dried, are considered spices.

Some even consider powdered milk and cheese, beef or chicken bouillon and dried bacon to be spices.

Herbs are usually the leaves of a plant and are used fresh. Herbs are, more often than not, more subtle in taste than spices. But when dried, they are considered to be a spice.

Some other items that you can use in spice blends - dried onion, dried peppers, salt, dried honey, hickory smoke flavoring, sugar, cocoa powder, coffee and dried veggies.

Spice Blends, Herbs, Rubs & Dip Mixes and Seasonings

Let's talk about the difference between spices, herbs, spice blends, rubs and dip mixes -

Spice Blends are just that - a blend of two or more spices.

Herbs are plant leaves - while spices are every other part of the plant including roots, stems, flowers, seeds and berries dried. This means that plants with edible leaves and seeds (like dill) are both herbs and spices.

Rubs are just mixtures of herbs and spices that you "rub" into meat before cooking. You can use any spice blend as a rub.

Dip mixes are blends of spices and herbs that you mix with sour cream, yogurt or mayonnaise. A dip mix can be used dry as a rub or spice blend and a rub or spice blend can be used as dip mix.

A spice blend or dip mix can be used as a salad dressing (ranch dressing mix).

So then, what is a *seasoning*? A seasoning is anything you put in food to add taste.

Is **salt** a spice? Salt is sold in the spice section of the grocery store. But salt is actually a mineral that is used as a flavor *enhancer*.

Tips for your spices

• Store them in a dark, dry, cool place in an airtight container. Not near stove or refrigerator.

• The shelf life for a whole product is 3 to 4 years, ground product is 2 to 3 years, and leafy product is 1 to 3 years.

• They won't go bad unless they get moist. But they will lose their potency and color.

• Don't ever let them get wet!

• Do not sprinkle spices directly from the bottle over the steaming pot. Steam cakes the contents and hastens the loss of flavor and aroma. In fact - just take those "sprinkle" tops off and throw them away!

• Make sure your measuring spoon is completely dry when you dip into a spice bottle. Any moisture will result in caking and flavor loss.

• If you need a "pinch" of a spice, make sure your hands are dry before pinching it out of the jar or bottle.

• If using spice to make a dip, let the dip sit at least an hour or two in the fridge before serving.

• Ground spices release their flavor quicker than whole spices. Use ground spices in recipes with a short cooking time, or add near end of longer cooking recipes. Whole spices (peppercorns, star anise) need more than twice as long as ground spices to release their flavor. Use whole products in soups and stews.

• Robust herbs such as sage, thyme and bay leaves stand up well in long cooking recipes. Milder herbs such as basil, marjoram and parsley should be added at the last minute for best results. Before adding to a recipe, rub leafy herbs in the palm of your hand to release their maximum flavor and aroma.

• Expose a spice's flavor by grinding or crushing it. Use a mortar & pestle, grinder or place them in a plastic bag and crush them with a rolling pin.

• Shake containers before opening.

- To expose flavor, heat spices in a dry skillet.

- Warm saffron for 10 seconds in the microwave then crush it to get the rich flavor out.

- When using spices the first time, start with a little until you see how much you like it.

- You'll need more spice on cold food than on hot food.

- If you make a dish and it turns out too spicy, try adding a little lemon juice, butter or vinegar.

- When making a dukkah grind it lightly by hand so it stays chunky.

Fun Things to Do With Spices -

Try cinnamon, ginger, cloves, anise or nutmeg in your coffee. Just add a little to the grounds before brewing. Or stir with cinnamon stick. In the Middle East they use cardamom in their coffee.

Add salt to coffee grounds to cut the bitter taste.

Boil carrots and puree them with a dash of curry powder for a soup. You can add coconut milk too.

Add poppy seeds to salad dressings.

Add turmeric to Dijon mustard.

Make tea from spices & herbs.

Infuse olive oil with a spice or spice blend.

Use a spice to infuse vodka.

Throw some spices or herbs into your bread mix (for example, Italian spice, beet powder, dill, garlic, even ground anise).

Some spices to sprinkle over eggs - chili, curry, paprika.

Many spice blends (and dip mixes) make a nice aioli when mixed with mayonnaise.

Sew little packets of herbs & spices to throw into your dryer so your clothes come out smelling good.

Use dried mint to get rid of ants.

Make an herbal bouquet from hibiscus, catnip, basil, lemongrass, peppermint, and/or lavender to get rid of flies & mosquitos.

~*~*~*~*~*~*~

Let's go over some spices that you may or may not have heard of or tried -

Ajwain seeds - Indian spice used in many dishes. Typically ground, these seeds have a strong fragrance with thyme and cumin undertones. They are used in Asian, Ethiopian, North Indian, Iranian, North Indian and Pakistani cuisines. They pair well with starchy foods like flatbreads, green beans, root vegetables and legumes. Ajwain seeds are excellent mixed with lemon and garlic with fish dishes. Substitute dried thyme.

Allspice - This individual spice is commonly confused to be a spice mixture but it is in fact a single spice. It has flavor tones of cloves, nutmeg, cinnamon and pepper. It is used in Jamaican Jerk seasoning and goes well when mixed with other, similar spices. Use it in spiced ciders and baking.

Almond Meal - (Not really a spice, but found in the spice section of some stores.) Almond Meal is made from un-blanched ground almonds. The consistency and application is similar to corn meal, but is not the same as almond flour.

Anise - Do not confuse with Star Anise. Anise is more often found ground. Anise seeds are small and look similar to dill or fennel seeds. Their aroma is sweet and licorice-like while their flavor is fruity and warm. They are most notably used in Italian pizzelles, Australian humbugs and Peruvian picarones. Used to make Italian cookies and biscotti. Try some on pizza!

Annatto or Achiote Seeds - Achiote is the name of the spice created from grinding Annatto seeds. This spice is typically used for coloring more than flavor but can be cooked in oil to infuse a little flavor. It has a flowery, peppermint aroma and is essential for making Yucatan Recado Rojo and achiote paste.

Arrowroot Powder - (Not really a spice, but found in the spice section of some stores.) Arrowroot is practically flavorless. Arrowroot powder is a gluten free starch that can be used to thicken sauces, clear glazes, gravies or pie fillings. It can be substituted anywhere flour or cornstarch is called for and to some, is considered to be superior to the two previously mentioned.

Asafoetida - Asafoetida is primarily used in Indian cooking. It has an strong onion-like scent. It is the gum-like material that comes from the root of several species of Ferula (a perennial herb). Once cooked it smells and tastes better.

Amchoor - Real amchoor is only made in India. It is a fruity powder made from dried unripe green mangoes and is used to give a citrusy flavor to Indian cooking. It's sometimes just called mango powder. Substitute lemon or lime.

Basil - Basil is somehow sweet yet savory at the same time. It has a peppery-anise flavor with minty undertones. Good in sauces, pesto, meats, soups and salads.

Bay leaves - Bay leaf is an aromatic spice. Bay has an earthy flavor with undertones of nutmeg and clove.

If using whole, always take out before serving - leaves can be sharp! It can be found in ground form also.

Beetroot Powder - (Not really a spice, but found in the spice section of some stores.) Beetroot Powder is used as both flavor and color foods. It is made from dehydrated beets, Beet Powder is sometimes added as a sweetener in juices or sauces.

Bell Peppers - Technically part of the chili pepper family, bell peppers come in a wide variety of colors and range in flavor from sweet to tart.

Cacao - Not to be confused with cocoa (hot chocolate). Cacao is the pure, unprocessed, dried seed of Theobrama cacao plant. It can be found as nibs or ground into a powder. The flavor is intense with a subtle mouth - cooling finish. Cacao is the ingredient that is emphasized in dark chocolate bars.

Caraway Seed - Caraway seed has a pungent aroma similar to dill and a sweet, warm, biting flavor that is like anise. It is generally used to make rye bread. It is also used in other foods like pickles, sauerkraut, sausages and cabbage soup.

Cardamom - Cardamom has a unique, lemony flavor, with an aroma that is biting and fruity. Cardamom can be used in its whole pod form or ground into a powder depending on the type of dish being prepared. Used in coffee in the Middle East. Add it to ice cream for a new flavor.

Celery Seed - Celery seeds and ground celery seed has a light "earthy" taste that is still fresh and. It comes from and tastes like celery.

Chervil - Chervil is more popular in France where it is used to make the blend Fines Herbs and in béarnaise sauce. It is related to parsley.

Chia Seeds - (Not really a spice, but found in the spice section of some stores.) Chia Seeds look similar to poppy seeds. When added to water they increase up to 12 times their original size. They contain more Omega-3 than any other natural source by volume. Their flavor is nutty but changes to slightly sweet when put into liquid. Chia seeds can be used in puddings, breads, oatmeal and jams.

Chiles - Chiles (as expected) add a level of heat to a dish. You can find them in a variety of forms - flakes, powdered and whole dried chilies. The heat level in of the chili depends on the type of chili used.

Chipotle - Chipotle is a dried, smoked jalapeno pepper. It can be found whole or powdered. Great for bar-b-que meats, soups and dips.

Cinnamon - Cinnamon is the oldest known spice. It actually comes from pieces of tree bark that have been sun dried. After drying, the bark is cut into strips or ground into a powder. Cinnamon comes from 4 parts of the world and each one has a slightly different flavor as well as oil content which determines its intensity - Mexico, Indonesia, Vietnam and China. Cinnamon is used in baking and can also be used in an variety of savory dishes such as chili, pasta sauce and stews.

Citrus Zests and Juice Powders - (Not really a spice, but found in the spice section of some stores.) Fruit zests are from the skin of citrus fruits, not including the white pith between the fruit and the peel. Zests are dried and can be reconstituted and used in baking recipes or powdered and mixed right into foods. They are now popular with beer brewers for beers that feature a fruity flavor. Juice powders are used in baking and cooking when a liquid component is not necessary.

Cloves - Cloves are probably the strongest spice that we use. They have a sweet yet bitter and somewhat astringent flavor. Whole cloves can be pushed right into food to add flavor (remove before serving). Clove oil is used for toothaches as it has a numbing effect. Cloves are used to flavor ham and pork, ciders and teas, in baking and in spice blends like pumpkin pie spice, Garam Masala and Chinese five spice.

Cocoa Powder (Black Onyx) - Cocoa powder is the processed, sweeter version of natural cacao. Black Onyx Cocoa Powder had an exceptionally smooth flavor. Cocoa powder is used in many drinks, desserts, mole and in steak rubs.

Coriander - The coriander plant produces both coriander seeds and the herb Cilantro. Coriander is popular in Mexican cooking, African food and in Indian dishes. It has a earthy flavor with citrusy undertones. It is also used to brew beer.

Cubeb Berry - Cubeb berries are not popular in the west but they have a distinct, intense flavor - kind of a mix between allspice and black pepper. They can be used in the like cloves or allspice.

Cumin - Cumin has a very distinct earthy, nutty and spicy flavor with a warm aroma with hints of lemon. It is a popular ingredient in many spice blends throughout Mexico and the Middle East and is used in rice dishes, beans (and chili), curry, and vegetable dishes.

Dill Seed or Weed - The dill plant produces both dill seeds and dill weed (an herb). It is probably most linked with the flavor of dill pickles. Dill's flavor is fresh, clean and pungent. In Scandinavian, German, and Russian cuisines it is a common spice used in cooking cabbage and potatoes. It is also good in yogurt with cucumbers.

Epazote - Epazote is a Mexican herb that gets similar reactions to cilantro when smelled and eaten - people who like it describe the flavor as earthy and bitter with hints of mint and citrus. Those who do not like epazote describe the flavor and aroma as similar to gasoline or turpentine. Epazote is used in traditional Mexican recipes including bean dishes, enchiladas and moles. It is a delicate herb, so it is often added near the end of the cooking.

Fennel - Fennel or fennel seeds are slightly sweet with a licorice aroma. It is used in potatoes, beets and other veggie dishes and meat dishes. Plus it adds flavor to sauerkraut.

Fenugreek - Fenugreek is popular in Indian and Middle Eastern dishes and is used in curry powders and other spice blends. It's strong flavor is nutty, spicy and a little bitter with undertones of sweet nuts. Fenugreek comes in seeds, leaves and powdered.

File Powder - Pronounced fee-lay. File powder is a spice made from dried, ground sassafras leaves. File powder is used in gumbo as both a flavoring and thickener. File powder can also be used to season seafood.

Galangal Root Powder - Galangal root powder is used in Southeast Asian cuisine. Galangal is similar to ginger but has a menthol flavor. Galangal goes well with beef and in curries and soups.

Garlic - Garlic is one of the most popular spices used in cooking around the world. It's flavor is pungent and strong. Garlic comes in granulated form and powdered. Also as a salt, but that's just garlic powder mixed with salt - make your own!

Ginger - The basic spice in gingerbread! Also a major spice in pumpkin pie spice blend. Ginger is actually the root of the ginger plant. Ground ginger is the root, - dried and powdered. Ginger is sweet, warm and some people say peppery flavored. It is used in teas and Asian cooking. Sprinkle a little on fish before cooking.

Grains of Paradise - Also known as seeds of paradise. Their flavor is peppery and pungent with bitter fruity notes and the aroma is similar to cardamom and clove. Grains of Paradise can be used in the same ways that peppercorns are used.

Horseradish Powder - (Also called Wasabi Powder) Horseradish Powder comes from the root of the horseradish plant. It has a "hot" flavor and is used to make wasabi in the U.S.   it's used in cocktail sauce and the root is ground to use with prime rib.

Juniper Berries - Juniper Berries come from an evergreen shrub that grows throughout the Northern Hemisphere. They have a tart, somewhat pine flavor. Juniper Berries are used in marinades for wild game and beef. They are also important for flavoring sauerkraut and gin.

Long Pepper - Long Pepper is now considered an exotic spice. It's similar to black pepper, but hotter.

Mace - You've heard of NUTMEG, right?   Nutmeg looks like a guava when it's growing. The Nutmeg is the seed inside and the *Mace* is the membrane that surrounds nutmeg. You can substitute nutmeg for mace, but it's flavor won't be as prominent.

Marjoram - Marjoram has a pungent and spicy or minty, sometime bitter flavor and can be used in any dish that you would include basil, oregano or thyme. It is an extremely versatile herb. Marjoram is used in salad dressings, soups, and poultry seasonings.

Malheb - Maleb is not popular in America but is used by the Greeks in baked goods. Mahlab is the dried kernel of the St. Lucie Cherry Tree. It has a delicate almond flavor with hints of cherries and roses. It works well in recipes combined with pistachios, rose water, apricots and dates.

Mustard - Mustard seeds come in yellow, brown and black. The darker the mustard seed, the more intense the flavor is when ground. Ground mustard is used for mustard sauces while whole mustard seeds are used for pickling.

Nigella Sativa - Nigella Seeds are popular in Middle Eastern and Indian cooking. They are usually roasted then ground and added to curries or vegetarian dishes. The seed itself has a little bit of a crunch which makes is a nice topping for flatbreads and breads.

Nutmeg - Nutmeg can be found as a powder or as a whole "nut" that you grate. It has a warm, sweet flavor. Nutmeg is used in baking, with lamb, in tomato sauces and vegetable stews. It's common to find it sprinkled in eggnog.

Onion - When used fresh onion is considered a vegetable but when it's dried and ground it is considered a spice. Onion is a very popular spice.

Oregano - Oregano is used mostly in tomato sauces. It is used in many Italian and Greek dishes. Great added to salad dressings or add a sprinkle to cooked vegetables.

Paprika - Paprika is a mild chili powder made from ground red bell peppers. It's used in Hungarian and Spanish dishes as well as a garnish. It has sweet, earthy flavor. You can find regular paprika, smoked paprika which is paprika that has been wood smoked and Hungarian paprika which is usually bright red and has a more pungent flavor.

Parsley - Fresh parsley is a popular garnish because of its beautiful green color. But dried, it has a nice vegetable flavor that is prominent in Middle Eastern recipes.

Pepper - Peppercorns come in black, green and white. They all come from the plant. The color differences depend on the maturity of the berries as well as the drying process used. White pepper is used when you are making a light dish and don't want dark specks in the food.

Pink peppercorns are not really peppercorns at all. They are berries from the Peruvian peppertree.

Poppy Seeds - Poppy seeds are teeny tiny seeds. They are so tiny that it takes 900,000 of them to make a pound. Poppy seeds taste nutty and add a crunch to salad dressings, vegetables, muffins and breads.

Porcini Powder - Porcini Powder is made from ground dried Porcini mushrooms and has a more concentrated flavor than just mushrooms. Porcini Powder can be used to add umami to a dish without using whole mushrooms.

Rosemary - Rosemary has a strong, kind of minty, almost eucalyptus flavor. Rosemary goes well with meats of all kinds, especially lamb, pork and wild game. It also makes a nice spread when mixed with butter or cream cheese. Or add it to your homemade bread dough.

Saffron - Because saffron production is so labor intensive, saffron is the most expensive and counterfeited spice in the world. Three to five pistils of a flower must be picked by hand. Saffron is used in a variety of applications including being a seasoning, fragrance, dye and medicine. The taste is light and sweet but powerful in cooking - you only need a little. Saffron is used in rice dishes along with broths and lamb. You can find cheaper varieties of "saffron flower" products, but they are not nearly as sweet or concentrated.

Savory - Savory's flavor is a cross between mint, marjoram and thyme. Savory is used in dishes such as beans, cabbage, potatoes, stews, and stuffing for meat pies. It is also used in pickling mixes.

Sage - Sage has a strong aroma and a savory, woodsy flavor that goes well with poultry. Sage is in many sausage recipes. Add to melted butter and use as a savory sauce for pasta.

Salt - Salt isn't really a spice it's a mineral. Spices add flavor, but salt enhances flavors. Salt comes in a range of shapes, sizes and colors. Very popular now is Himalayan Pink Salt which has 84 trace minerals. Sea salt is also popular. Smoked salts are actually smoked over wood to give it a smoky flavor.

Sesame Seeds - (Not really a spice, but found in the spice section of some stores.) Tiny as they are, sesame seeds pack a lot of flavor. They come in white, black and red. The black are a bit stronger in flavor. They are popular in Chinese dishes and Middle Eastern spice blends. Sesame Seeds can also be used in baked goods and salads.

Star Anise - Star Anise is not the same as anise seed. Star anise is a spice that has a shape similar to a star and typically has 8 points, but can have more or less. In the United States star anise is used similarly to cloves in application. The whole pods are used as mulling spices and the ground pod is used in baking and cold weather beverages.

Sumac - Sumac is from dried sumac berries. It's a bright reddish purple and has a fruity tart flavor that is like vinegar or citrus but not as strong as lemon. You can use sumac powder in any dish that you would use lemon juice in. It's used in the Middle East and India.

Szechuan Pepper - This pepper is used mostly in Chinese cooking. It has a unique flavor that numbs the tongue and lips. Kind of a combo of cloves, lemon and pepper.

Tarragon - Tarragon is used a lot in French cooking. It's flavor sweet, light and warm. It is a key ingredient in the herb blend Herbs de Provence. Tarragon works well blended with dill, parsley, chives and basil and can be used to flavor vegetables, poultry, mushrooms, eggs and seafood.

Thyme - Thyme has a fresh yet strong, lemony flavor. It is used in sauces, vinegars, soups and uses widely in Creole cooking to add flavor to blackened meats and fish. Thyme is used in widely for poultry including in turkey stuffing.

Turmeric - Turmeric is a root kind of like ginger. It has many health benefits. Turmeric has an earthy flavor and is a main ingredient in masalas, Ras el Hanout and curries. It's bright yellow color lends itself to be used as a natural coloring for foods.

Vanilla Powder - (Not really a spice, but found in the spice section of some stores.) Vanilla comes from a bean. Vanilla powder is the bean, dried and ground. It has no sugar or alcohol so is preferred by some to the liquid extract. Nice to use if you don't want to add liquid to a dish. Guinea and Uganda, although these types are lesser known. Vanilla is commonly used for making desserts, beverages and liquors.

Spice Flavor Categories

Spices break down into 5 flavor categories - sweet, hot, pungent, spicy and savory. Some people claim there are more categories and some claim less. A few of the others are smoky, bitter and fruity.

As I mentioned in the introduction, **Chinese Five Spice** is a traditional spice blend, named after the five flavor categories (spicy, savory, hot, sweet, pungent). The combination of these flavors is thought to create balance.

I invite you to use the formula below to make your own signature spice blend. Check out the different spices in each category, pick the ones you like and make a blend. After you've made one, alter any ingredients (use less of those you don't like and more of the ones you like a lot!) and see how that one turns out.

Five Category Recipe

Amalgamating (Savory) (10 teaspoons): coriander, cumin, fennel, oregano, paprika, poppy seeds, rosemary, sesame seeds, paprika, thyme and turmeric.

Hot (1 teaspoon): chili, horseradish, mace, mustard, peppers and wasabi.

Pungent (1 teaspoon): bay leaf, caraway, cardamom, celery seeds, cloves, cumin, dill, fenugreek, garlic, juniper, mace, onion and star anise.

Sweet (4 teaspoons): allspice, anise, cinnamon, fennel, mint, nutmeg and vanilla powder.

Tangy (2 teaspoon): amchur (dried green mango powder), barberry, black lime, caper, galangal, ginger, pomegranate, suman and tamarind.

Spice Blend Recipes

Following are the recipes for some very popular spice blends. I've also listed the country from which they came if applicable. They are listed in alphabetical order.

Alter the recipes to your taste. Use more of what you like and less of what you don't like.

Most recipes have ideas of how to use them. And after this section there are recipes for dishes to use some of these spice blends in. Enjoy!

ACOG Season Salt

Mix together 4 teaspoons of each of the following -

Sea Salt	Black Pepper
Anise	Dried Orange Peel
Coriander	Powdered Ginger

Experiment!
- Use lime powder instead of orange peel
- Use cumin in place of coriander
- Use chili powder instead of pepper

This is great on fish, veggies (especially sliced cucumbers), meat, and works as a table salt. If you use this in place of salt, you'll use 1/6 of the salt you usually use.

Adobo Spice Blend - *Portugal*

1/4 cup sweet paprika
3 tablespoons ground black pepper
2 tablespoons onion powder
2 tablespoons dried oregano

2 tablespoons ground cumin
1 tablespoon chipotle chili powder
1 tablespoon garlic powder
1 teaspoon turmeric

Mix all ingredients together well. Store in airtight container.

How to use:

Use as a dry rub for any meat, especially chicken.
Add olive oil to make a sauce.
Put spice blend in soups, eggs or sprinkle on chicken or fish.
Add 1 tablespoon to 4 ounces mayonnaise and 12 ounces sour cream. Add
the juice of a lime. Then use as a crema for tacos or nachos.
Use adobo to season guacamole, tacos, chili meat, or beans.

Advieh - *Persia*

1 teaspoon ground cinnamon
1 teaspoon ground nutmeg
1 teaspoon ground cardamom
½ teaspoon ground cumin

1 teaspoon ground turmeric
1 teaspoon ground coriander
1 teaspoon ground rose petal

Mix all ingredients together well. Store in airtight container.

How to use:

Use in lamb & split pea stew.
Put in soups, chicken dishes or rice pilaf.
Great on grilled or roasted veggies.
Add a pinch to an omelet.
Also used in rice pudding.

Arabic Spice - *Middle East*

2 tablespoons paprika
2 tablespoons ground cumin
1 tablespoon ground coriander
1 teaspoon ground turmeric
1 teaspoon ground ginger
1 tablespoon ground black pepper

½ teaspoon ground nutmeg
½ teaspoon ground cinnamon
½ teaspoon ground anise
½ teaspoon ground cardamom
½ teaspoon ground clove

Mix all ingredients together well. Store in airtight container.

How to use:
Use as a dry rub on lamb or other meats, especially on shish kabob.
Use in soups & stews.
Sprinkle on carrots and beef or lamb roast.

Bacon & Chili Cheese Dip Mix - *America*

2 tablespoons bacon chips or dried bacon
1- ½ tablespoon minced onion
1-1/4 teaspoons garlic powder
2-1/2 teaspoons cheddar cheese powder

1-1/4 teaspoons chili powder
1/2 teaspoons cumin
1/4 tsp salt
1/4 tsp cayenne pepper

Mix all ingredients together well. Store in airtight container.

To serve:
Mix 2 tablespoons dip mix with 2 cups sour cream or 1 cup sour cream and 1 cup mayonnaise. Stir until well blended. Cover and refrigerate for at least 2 hours before serving. Serve with chips, crackers or veggies.

Baharat Spice - *Middle East*

1 tablespoon black pepper
1 tablespoon cumin
2 teaspoons coriander
1 teaspoon cloves
½ teaspoon cardamom

1½ tablespoons paprika
1 teaspoons ground cinnamon
¼ teaspoon ground nutmeg
1 tablespoon allspice

Mix all ingredients together well. Store in airtight container.

Mix some into ground lamb and make as burgers or kabobs. Sprinkle on fish before cooking. Mix 1 tablespoon into 1 cup of hummus for a tasty dip.

Also use to season fish, chicken, beef, and soups. Mix into ground lamb, grill and serve in pita bread.

BBQ Pit Dukkah - *America*

1 cup smoked almonds
1 tablespoon garlic salt
2 tablespoons dried onion flakes
dash of chili flakes

1 teaspoon smoked sea salt
1 teaspoon dried mustard
2 teaspoons dried orange peel

Gently grind all ingredients together. Store in airtight container until ready to use.

To use:
Pour some over a block of cream cheese and serve with crackers (like a cheese ball).

Bar-B-Q Rub - America

½ cup brown sugar
½ cup paprika
1 tablespoon ground black pepper
1 tablespoon kosher or sea salt
1 teaspoon dry mustard

1 tablespoon chili powder
1 tablespoon garlic powder
1 tablespoon onion powder

Mix all ingredients together well. Store in airtight container.

Rub onto meats or chicken at least one hour before grilling. Sprinkle on burgers before cooking. also great on ribs or pork chops. Add to muffin or bread mixes.

Beet Dip Mix - *Australia*

¼ cup beetroot powder
1 teaspoon garlic powder
1 teaspoon onion powder
1 teaspoon sumac
1 teaspoon parsley
1 teaspoon cumin

1 teaspoon dried chives
1 teaspoon paprika
1 teaspoon coriander
1 teaspoon cinnamon
1 teaspoon pepper

Mix all ingredients together well. Store in airtight container.

To use:
Mix 2 tablespoons dip mix with 2 cups sour cream or 1 cup sour cream and 1 cup mayonnaise. Stir until well blended. Cover and refrigerate for at least 2 hours before serving. Serve with chips, crackers or veggies.

Other uses - mix into cake or cookie mixes, frostings or add a little to hot cereals,

Berbere - *Ethiopia*

1/4 teaspoon fenugreek
8 teaspoons ground chili powder
5 teaspoons paprika
1/2 tablespoon salt
1/2 teaspoon ground ginger
1/4 teaspoon onion powder
1/2 teaspoon ground cardamom

1 teaspoon ground coriander
1/4 teaspoon ground nutmeg
1/4 teaspoon garlic powder
1/8 teaspoon ground cloves
1/8 teaspoon ground cinnamon
1/8 teaspoon ground allspice

Mix all ingredients together well. Store in airtight container.

Berbere is a warm spice blend with a chili base. It combines sweet, bitter and spicy tastes. It's an all-purpose spice mix that is used in soups, stews, vegetables and all types of dishes. Sprinkle some in mac & cheese or blend with melted butter to use on corn on the cob.

Biryani Spice Blend - *India*

2 teaspoons ground cumin
2 teaspoons ground coriander
2 teaspoons ground turmeric
1 teaspoon ground ginger
1 teaspoon ground cinnamon
1 teaspoon freshly ground pepper
1 teaspoon freshly ground nutmeg

1 teaspoon ground cardamom
½ teaspoon onion powder
½ teaspoon garlic powder
½ teaspoon dried mint
½ teaspoon bay leaf
½ teaspoon anise
½ teaspoon ground cloves

Mix all ingredients together well. Store in airtight container.

* See Chicken Biryani recipe in the *Recipes* section in this book.

Chaat Masala - *India*

1-1/3 tablespoons ground cumin
2-2/3 teaspoons ground coriander
1-1/3 teaspoons pepper
2 teaspoons salt

Mix all ingredients together well. Store in airtight container.

To Use -
Sprinkle on veggies, main dishes, rice and pasta dishes.

Chili, Lime Chipotle Rub - *America*

2 tablespoons lime powder
1 teaspoon to 1 tablespoon chipotle spice
2 teaspoons chili powder
2 teaspoons garlic powder

1 teaspoon onion powder
1 teaspoon coriander
1 teaspoon dried cilantro
Pinch of salt
¼ teaspoon black pepper

Mix all ingredients together well. Store in airtight container.

To Use -

Rub onto steaks, chicken or fish at least one hour before grilling.

Chili Seasoning

Make this your own by using more or less of an ingredient. Also, use different kinds of pepper or chilies.

Basic Recipe

4 tablespoons paprika

4 teaspoons oregano

3 to 4 teaspoons cayenne or other pepper

2 to 3 teaspoons cumin

2 teaspoons garlic powder

1 teaspoons onion powder

1/2 teaspoon cinnamon

1/2 teaspoon sugar

Mix all ingredients together well. Store in airtight container.

Coconut Spice Blend - *Sri Lanka*

1 cup dried unsweetened coconut

2 tablespoons lime powder

1 tablespoon garlic powder

1 tablespoon onion powder

1 tablespoon turmeric

1 tablespoon ginger

1 teaspoon fennel

1 teaspoon black pepper

1 teaspoon cinnamon

1/2 teaspoon red chili flakes

1/2 teaspoon salt

Place all items in a zip-lock plastic bag and hammer with a mallet to crush the ingredients together. Store in airtight container.

* See Sri Lankan Coconut Chicken recipe in the *Recipes* section in this book.

Curry Powder - *India*

2 tablespoons ground coriander
2 tablespoons ground cumin
1 1/2 tablespoons ground turmeric
2 teaspoons ground ginger
1 teaspoon dry mustard
1/2 teaspoon ground black pepper

1 teaspoon ground cinnamon
1/2 teaspoon ground cardamom
1/2 teaspoon cayenne pepper
1/2 teaspoon cloves
1/2 teaspoon nutmeg

Mix all ingredients together well. Store in airtight container.

Use this spice blend as you would any curry powder.

You can use curry powder as an all-purpose seasoning. It is commonly used to flavor soups, stews, sauces, rice dishes, marinades, meat, and vegetables. Sprinkle some Curry Powder into the mixture the next time you make deviled eggs.

Curry Dip Mix - India

1 tablespoon dried parsley
2 teaspoons minced onion
2 teaspoons dried chives
1 teaspoon onion powder
1-1/2 teaspoons garlic powder

1 teaspoon celery salt
1/2 teaspoon curry powder
1/8 teaspoon turmeric
1/8 teaspoon cumin
1/2 teaspoon salt

Mix all ingredients together well. Store in airtight container.

To use:
Mix 2 tablespoons dip mix with 2 cups sour cream or 1 cup sour cream and 1 cup mayonnaise. Stir until well blended. Cover and refrigerate for at least 2 hours before serving. Serve with chips, crackers or veggies.

Also good added to deviled eggs, white sauces, potato salad or in pumpkin or squash soup.

Dill & Onion Dip Mix - *America*

4 tablespoons dried onion
1-1/2 tablespoons dill
2 teaspoons parsley

½ teaspoon garlic powder
½ teaspoon celery seed
1 teaspoon salt

Mix all ingredients together well. Store in airtight container.

To use:
Mix 2 tablespoons dip mix with 2 cups sour cream or 1 cup sour cream and 1 cup mayonnaise. Stir until well blended. Cover and refrigerate for at least 2 hours before serving. Serve with chips, crackers or veggies.
This dip makes a delicious dipping sauce for meatballs or kabobs.

Add dry mix to Greek yogurt and cucumbers to make tzatziki. Or add it to falafel. Add dry mix to cream cheese and spread on toast or bagels with lox.

Egyptian Dukkah - *Egypt*

4 tablespoons sesame seeds, toasted
3 tablespoons coriander seeds, toasted
3 tablespoons pistachios, toasted
3 tablespoons cashews, toasted

1 tablespoon cumin seeds, toasted
½ tablespoon fennel seeds, toasted
1 teaspoon kosher salt
1 teaspoon dried mint
1/2 teaspoon sugar
Pinch red pepper flakes

Combine all ingredients in a zippered plastic bag. Using a mallet or rolling pin, crush items and mix together. Store in airtight container until ready to use.

To use:
Pour some over a block of cream cheese and serve with crackers (like a cheese ball). Or - set out with slices of crusty bread and a bowl of olive oil. Dip bread into oil then into dukkah.

Emperor's Garden Dip Mix - *China*

2 tablespoons dried carrot
2 tablespoons dried red bell
peppers
2 tablespoons dried chives
2 tablespoons sesame seeds
2 tablespoons onion powder
2 tablespoons garlic powder
2 tablespoons dried cilantro

2 tablespoons ginger
2 tablespoons orange peel powder
or dried peel
1 tablespoon dried mustard
1 tablespoon dried basil
1 teaspoon black pepper
1 teaspoon cayenne powder

Mix all ingredients together well. Store in airtight container.

To use:
Mix 2 tablespoons dip mix with 2 cups sour cream or 1 cup sour cream and 1 cup mayonnaise. Stir until well blended. Cover and refrigerate for at least 2 hours before serving. Serve with chips, crackers or veggies.

Everything Bagel Spice Blend - America

2 ½ teaspoons poppy seeds
2 ½ teaspoons of sesame seeds
1 teaspoon of salt

2 teaspoons dried minced garlic
2 teaspoons dried onion flakes

Mix all ingredients together well. Store in airtight container.

Use to top homemade bagels. Also good as a topping or ingredient for biscuits or muffins.

Spoon over a block of cream cheese and use as a spread for crackers or bagels.

Five Spice - *China*

1 teaspoon ground cinnamon
1 teaspoon ground cloves
1 teaspoon fennel seed, toasted
and ground

1 teaspoon ground star anise
1 teaspoon Szechuan peppercorns,
toasted and ground
1 teaspoon crushed sesame seeds

Mix all ingredients together well. Store in airtight container.

A staple in most Chinese cooking. Use as a spice for duck, goose, pork and chicken. Good in beef & broccoli. Add to ketchup for great Asian flavor.

Furikake - *Japan*

1/2 cup toasted sesame seeds
1 teaspoon to 1 tablespoon sea salt
to taste

3 sheets nori
3 heaping tablespoons bonito flakes
1/2 teaspoon sugar

Use kitchen shears or clean, dry scissors to cut the nori into 1-inch strips. Stack the strips and cut cross-wise into very thin squares over the bowl of sesame seeds. Use the kitchen shears again to roughly cut up the bonito flakes, if needed. Mix all ingredients together. Store in airtight container.

Furikake is meant to be sprinkled on top of cooked rice, sushi and bento lunch box but it's also good on eggs, vegetables and fish.

Garam Masala - *India*

1 tablespoon ground cumin
1 1/2 teaspoons ground coriander
1 1/2 teaspoons ground cardamom
1 1/2 teaspoons ground black
pepper

1 1/2 teaspoon ground cinnamon
1/2 teaspoon ground cloves
1/2 teaspoon ground nutmeg
1/2 teaspoon anise

Mix all ingredients together well. Store in airtight container.

Use in most Indian cooking. Sprinkle on slices of eggplant and broil.
Great on baked or sweet potatoes. Mix some into mayonnaise for a delicious,
exotic sandwich spread. Try using some in soups or veggies. Season chicken
with Garam Masala. Also good sprinkled over popcorn.

* See Tikka Masala recipe in the *Recipes* section in this book.

Gingerbread Spice Mix - *America*

1/2 cup cinnamon
1/2 cup ground ginger
1/4 cup allspice

1/4 cup nutmeg
1/4 cup ground cloves
A pinch of black pepper

Mix all ingredients together well. Store in airtight container.

For standard size cakes (9" x 13" or two 8" rounds) use 5 teaspoons of the mix.
For a standard size cookie recipe (2 to 3 dozen), use 4 teaspoons of the mix.
To flavor ground coffee before brewing, use 1 to 2 teaspoons of the mix.
For pancakes or waffles, use 2 to 3 teaspoons of the mix to flavor batter that is
meant to make a dozen or so servings.
Mix with sugar and sprinkle over buttered toast for a new version of cinnamon
toast.

Golden Milk (Turmeric Tea)

1/4 cup sugar or stevia
1/3 cup turmeric
1/4 cup cinnamon

1/4 cup ground ginger
1 teaspoon of black pepper

Mix all ingredients together well. Store in airtight container.

To make golden milk, mix 2 tablespoons of the mix into 1 cup of any kind of hot milk (cow's, almond, soy, etc.). Sprinkle cinnamon on top if you wish. If not sweet enough, add a little honey to milk.

Greek Spice Mix - *Greece*

2 teaspoons garlic powder
2 teaspoons dried oregano
2 teaspoons mint
1-1/2 teaspoons onion powder garlic
1 teaspoon basil
1 teaspoon marjoram

1 teaspoon salt
1 teaspoon dill
1 teaspoon rosemary
1/2 teaspoon thyme
1/2 teaspoon ground cinnamon
1/2 teaspoon ground nutmeg

Mix all ingredients together well. Store in airtight container.

Add this spice blend to vinegar for a delicious salad dressing.
* See Greek Avgolemono Soup recipe in the *Recipes* section in this book.

Harissa Seasoning Spice - *North Africa*

4 ounces dried chilies of your choice
2 tablespoons garlic powder
1 tablespoon dried lemon peel
1 tablespoon dried mint

1 teaspoon caraway seeds
1 teaspoon coriander seeds
1 teaspoon cumin seeds
1 teaspoon kosher salt
1 teaspoon paprika

Grind all ingredients into a powder.

To make paste add 2 tablespoons extra virgin olive oil and 4 tablespoons tomato paste. If it's too thick add a little fresh lemon juice or olive oil. Optional addition: sun-dried tomatoes.
Use on meats, in shakshuka, or as a dip for chicken wings.

Herb & Garlic Dip Mix - *America*

2 tablespoons dried parsley
2 teaspoons minced onion
1 teaspoon sugar
1/2 teaspoon dried oregano

1/2 teaspoon dried basil
1/2 teaspoon dried thyme
1/2 teaspoon garlic powder
1/4 teaspoon black pepper

Mix all ingredients together well. Store in airtight container.

To use:
Mix 2 tablespoons dip mix with 2 cups sour cream or 1 cup sour cream and 1 cup mayonnaise. Stir until well blended. Cover and refrigerate for at least 2 hours before serving. Serve with chips, crackers or veggies.

Sprinkle onto garlic bread or on chicken before cooking.

Cheesy Herb & Garlic Dip Mix - *America*

Add 4 tablespoons grated parmesan cheese to the above recipe.

Italian Seasoning - *Italy*

2 tablespoons basil
2 tablespoons marjoram
2 tablespoons oregano

2 tablespoons rosemary
2 tablespoons thyme
1 to 2 tablespoons garlic powder

Mix all ingredients together well. Store in airtight container.

Mix into balsamic vinegar for a yummy salad dressing.   Sprinkle over pasta or add to pasta sauce. Mix into ground beef for an Italian meatloaf or meatballs.

Jerk Spice Blend - *Jamaica*

1 tablespoon garlic powder
1 Tablespoon dried thyme
2 to 3 teaspoons cayenne pepper
2 teaspoons onion powder
2 teaspoons dried thyme
2 teaspoons dried parsley
2 teaspoons brown sugar
1 teaspoon salt

1 teaspoon paprika
1 teaspoon ground allspice
1/2 teaspoon black pepper
1/2 teaspoon dried crushed red pepper
1/2 teaspoon ground nutmeg
1/4 teaspoon ground cinnamon

Mix all ingredients together well. Store in airtight container.

* See Caribbean Jerk Chicken recipe in the *Recipes* section in this book.

Lime Cracked Pepper Salt - *Australia*

4 teaspoons granulated lime zest or lime powder

4 teaspoons black peppercorns
4 teaspoons coarse sea salt

Mix all ingredients together well. Store in airtight container or place in a pepper mill. Grind it as you need it. (Always shake first!)

Louisiana Creole Spice or Dip Mix - America

3 tablespoons onion powder
3 tablespoons garlic powder
1 ½ tablespoons black pepper
1 ½ tablespoons white pepper
6 tablespoons paprika

½ - 1 tablespoons cayenne pepper
1 1/2 tablespoons oregano
1 tablespoon dried parsley
1 1/2 tablespoons dried thyme
1 1/2 tablespoons dried basil

Mix all ingredients together well. Store in airtight container.

Mix 2 tablespoons dip mix with 2 cups sour cream or 1 cup sour cream and 1 cup mayonnaise. Stir until well blended. Cover and refrigerate for at least 2 hours before serving. Cover and refrigerate for at least 2 hours before serving. Serve with chips, crackers or veggies.

Also use in soups and stews, rice dishes and on meat or fish.

Marrakesh Moroccan Spice Blend - *Morocco*

1 teaspoon ground cumin
1 teaspoon ground ginger
1 teaspoon ground nutmeg
3/4 teaspoon black pepper
1/2 teaspoon ground cinnamon

1/2 teaspoon ground coriander
1/2 teaspoon cayenne pepper
1/2 teaspoon salt
1/2 teaspoon ground allspice
1/4 teaspoon ground cloves

Mix all ingredients together well. Store in airtight container.

Give an authentic African flavor to meats and soups with this spice blend. Especially good in lamb.

* See Marrakesh Vegetable Curry recipe in the *Recipes* section in this book.

Mexican Spice Blend - *Mexico*

1 tablespoon ground cumin
1 tablespoon dried coriander leaves
1 tablespoon mild paprika

1 teaspoon ground oregano
1/2 teaspoon chili powder
1/2 teaspoon garlic powder

Mix all ingredients together well. Store in airtight container.

Use in ground meat for tacos, enchiladas, and other Mexican foods. Also good in soups and casseroles.

Mongolian Dip Mix - Mongolia

1 tablespoon dried bell pepper
1 tablespoon garlic powder
1 tablespoon onion powder
2 teaspoons dried cilantro
2 teaspoons dried ginger
1 to 2 teaspoons cayenne powder

1 teaspoon sumac
1 teaspoon paprika
1 teaspoon Szechuan pepper (or
    substitute black pepper)
1 teaspoon sugar
1 teaspoon salt

Mix all ingredients together well. Store in airtight container.

* See Mongolian Beef recipe in the *Recipes* section in this book.
Also use in soups and stews, rice dishes and on meat or fish.

Mix 2 tablespoons dip mix with 2 cups sour cream or 1 cup sour cream and 1 cup mayonnaise. Stir until well blended. Cover and refrigerate for at least 2 hours before serving.

Mulling Spice Blend - *America*

4 teaspoons whole allspice
1/2 teaspoon whole cloves
2 (3 x 1-inch) strips orange rind

2 (3-inch) cinnamon sticks, broken in half

Place items in a zip-close storage bag. Pound with a mallet to break up. Store mixture in a tightly closed jar.

When ready to use, tie about ¼ of the mixture into a gauze bag or reusable tea bag. You can also put mixture into gauze bags and give as holiday gifts.

Steep in hot cider, tea or wine.

Simmer 12 ounces of maple syrup and a spice bag over low heat for 5 minutes. Cover and chill for 24 hours. Discard the spice bag. Store in refrigerator up to 2 weeks. Serve warm with pancakes or waffles.

Simmer 16 ounces of apple cider vinegar and a spice bag for 1 minute. Remove from heat and let stand for 3 hours. Discard bag. Store up to 2 weeks as a vinaigrette to toss with salads.

Onion Soup & Dip Mix - *America*

4 teaspoons beef bouillon granules
2 tablespoons dried minced onions
1 teaspoon onion powder
¼ teaspoon freshly ground black

pepper
½ teaspoon sugar
½ teaspoon dried parsley

Mix all ingredients together well. Store in airtight container.

Mix 2 tablespoons dip mix with 2 cups sour cream or 1 cup sour cream and 1 cup mayonnaise. Stir until well blended. Cover and refrigerate for at least 2 hours before serving.

Add to meatloaf or meatball mix. Use in soups.

Peri Peri Spice Blend - *Portugal*

1½ teaspoons paprika
1 teaspoon dried oregano, crushed
1 teaspoon ground ginger
1 teaspoon ground cardamom
1 teaspoon garlic powder

1 teaspoon onion powder
1⁄2 teaspoon salt
1⁄2 chipotle pepper
½ teaspoon cinnamon

Mix all ingredients together well. Store in airtight container.

Peri Peri is usually a sauce. But you can use this spice blend dry on meats or add some red wine vinegar and lemon juice to create a Peri Peri sauce.

* See Peri Peri Chicken recipe in the *Recipes* section in this book.

Poultry Spice Blend - *America*

1 tablespoon ground sage
1 tablespoon ground thyme
1 tablespoon ground marjoram
1 teaspoon ground rosemary

1 teaspoon crushed celery seed
1 teaspoon ground black pepper
1 teaspoon nutmeg

Mix all ingredients together well. Store in airtight container.

Of course, you'll want this seasoning for turkey stuffing, but also try adding a teaspoon full to soups, casseroles, veggies or rice.

Make a meatloaf from ground turkey and add this spice blend to it.

Pulled Pork Meat Rub - *America*

1/2 cup smoked paprika
1/3 cup dark brown sugar
1/4 cup salt
1/4 cup garlic powder
2 tablespoons black pepper
2 tablespoons chili powder

2 tablespoons onion powder
2 tablespoons chipotle chili pepper
1 tablespoon cayenne pepper
1 tablespoon cumin
1 tablespoon dry mustard

Mix all ingredients together well. Store in airtight container.

Rub onto pork before cooking. Try it on other meats too!

Pumpkin Fiesta Dip Mix - *Mexico*

1 cup pumpkin powder
2 tablespoons dried red bell pepper
2 tablespoons dried onion flakes
2 tablespoons dried black olives
1 tablespoon dried chives
1 tablespoon garlic powder
2 teaspoons oregano
1 teaspoon cinnamon
1 teaspoon cumin
1 teaspoon smoked paprika

1 teaspoon ginger
1 teaspoon chipotle powder
1 teaspoon dried lime zest
½ teaspoon nutmeg
½ teaspoon allspice
½ teaspoon cloves
½ teaspoon sage
¼ teaspoon salt
¼ teaspoon sugar

Mix all ingredients together well. Store in airtight container.

Mix 2 tablespoons dip mix with 2 cups sour cream or 1 cup sour cream and 1 cup mayonnaise. Stir until well blended. Cover and refrigerate for at least 2 hours before serving.

Add to meatloaf or meatball mix or to soups.

Pumpkin Pie Spice - *America*

3 tablespoons ground cinnamon
2 teaspoons ground ginger
1-1/2 teaspoon ground allspice

1-1/2 teaspoon ground cloves
2 teaspoons nutmeg
1/2 teaspoon ground mace

Mix all ingredients together well. Store in airtight container.

Use this in lots of fall or winter baking. Put it in cookie dough, cheesecake or pumpkin pancakes. Mix a spoon or two into whipped cream and use as frosting or to dip fruit into. Add it to coffee grounds before brewing. Delicious sprinkled onto baked sweet potatoes.

Ranch Dressing Mix - America

1/2 cup dry buttermilk powder
1 tablespoon dried parsley
2 teaspoons dried dill weed
1 teaspoon freeze dried chives

1 tablespoon garlic powder
1 tablespoon onion powder
1 teaspoon sea salt
1/2 teaspoon ground black pepper

Mix all ingredients together well. Store in refrigerator in an airtight container.

Homemade Ranch Dip
Mix together ¼ cup of ranch seasoning mix with 1 cup of sour cream and 2 tablespoons buttermilk.

Homemade Ranch Dressing
Mix together ¼ cup ranch seasoning mix with 1 cup mayonnaise, ½ cup sour cream, and ½ cup buttermilk.

Ranch Popcorn
Toss melted butter onto popcorn or spray with non-stick cooking spray. Sprinkle in 1 to 2 tablespoons of ranch seasoning mix.

Roasted Ranch Potato Wedges
Toss 1 pound of potato wedges with 2 tablespoons olive oil and 1 tablespoon ranch seasoning mix. Roast at 400ºF for about 30 minutes, until tender.

Ras El Hanout Spice Blend - *Morocco*

2 teaspoons ground nutmeg
2 teaspoons ground coriander
2 teaspoons ground cumin
2 teaspoons ground ginger
2 teaspoons turmeric
2 teaspoons salt
2 teaspoons cinnamon
1 1⁄2 teaspoons sugar

1 1⁄2 teaspoons paprika
1 1⁄2 teaspoons ground black pepper
1 teaspoon cayenne pepper
1 teaspoon cardamom powder
1 teaspoon ground allspice
1⁄2 teaspoon ground cloves

Mix all ingredients together well. Store in airtight container.

This blend is convenient to use in marinades, as a rub, as a seasoning in many dishes like stews and soups. It's also great on salmon.

Mix Ras el Hanout with softened butter or sour cream to instantly make an interesting topping for baked potatoes, or toss it on popcorn for a savory snack.

* See Moroccan Chicken and Onion Tagine recipe in the *Recipes* section in this book.

Ras El Hanout Spice Blend #2 - *North Africa*

2 teaspoons ground ginger
2 teaspoons ground cardamom
2 teaspoons ground mace
1 teaspoon cinnamon
1 teaspoon ground allspice
1 teaspoon ground coriander seeds
1 teaspoon ground nutmeg

1 teaspoon turmeric
1/2 teaspoon ground black pepper
1/2 teaspoon ground white pepper
1/2 teaspoon ground cayenne pepper
1/2 teaspoon ground anise seeds
1/4 teaspoon ground cloves

Mix all ingredients together well. Store in airtight container.

Use as above.

Rendang Spice Blend - *Indonesia*

1-1/2 tablespoons coriander seeds
1-1/2 tablespoons garlic powder
1 tablespoon cinnamon
1 tablespoon fennel seeds
1 tablespoon cumin seeds
2 teaspoons cardamom

1 teaspoon anise
1 teaspoon onion powder
½ teaspoon cumin
½ teaspoon turmeric
½ teaspoon ground ginger

Mix all ingredients together well. Store in airtight container.

Beef Rendang is a very complicated meal to cook. But with this spice blend and some coconut cream you can imitate it.

Seafood Seasoning Blend - *America*

6.3 tablespoons salt
3.3 tablespoons ground celery seed
2.5 teaspoons dry mustard powder
2.5 teaspoons red pepper flakes, ground
1.5 teaspoons ground black pepper

1.5 teaspoons ground bay leaves
1.5 teaspoons paprika
1 teaspoon ground cloves
1 teaspoon ground allspice
1 teaspoon ground ginger
3/4 teaspoon ground cardamom
1/2 teaspoon ground cinnamon

Mix all ingredients together well. Store in airtight container.

Great on fish of all kinds.

Seasoned Salt

4 tablespoons salt

1/2 teaspoon onion powder

1/2 teaspoon garlic powder

1/2 teaspoon ground black pepper

1 teaspoon paprika

1⁄4 teaspoon turmeric

1/2 teaspoon chili powder (optional)

2 tablespoons dried parsley leaf (optional)

1 teaspoon sugar (optional)

Mix ingredients together. Change as needed - variations:

- o Add more or less of anything above
- o Leave out the salt for a salt free "season salt"
- o Leave out the sugar
- o Add some turmeric
- o Add some cumin
- o Add in some cinnamon

"Steakhouse" Season Salt

This recipe is fashioned after famous steak restaurants and their season salts are sold in grocery stores.

1/4 cup salt

1/4 cup sugar

1 teaspoon paprika

1⁄2 teaspoon turmeric

1⁄2 teaspoon onion powder

1⁄2 teaspoon garlic powder

Mix ingredients together. Adjust ingredients as needed.

Supeq Spice Blend - *Native American*

(Supeq means ocean)

¼ cup seaweed, diced
¼ cup dried shiitake mushroom, crushed
1/8 cup ginger powder

1/8 cup dried nettle
1/8 cup smoked paprika
1 teaspoon sea salt

Mix all ingredients together well. Store in airtight container.

Try on top of eggs or fish, mix into kale salad or sautéed spinach, or just sprinkle on popcorn.

Sweet & Smoky BBQ Rub - *America*

1/2 teaspoon ground chipotle chili
2 teaspoon dried rosemary
1/2 teaspoon thyme
1/2 teaspoon mustard powder
1/4 teaspoon ground allspice
1 teaspoon black pepper

1/4 cup dark brown sugar
2 teaspoons chili powder
2 tablespoons kosher salt or coarse sea salt
1 1/3 tablespoons smoked paprika
1 teaspoon cumin

Mix all ingredients together well. Store in airtight container.

Rub into beef or chicken and let sit in the fridge to marinate for at least 1 hour. Then cook as usual.

Taco Seasoning - *America*

Make this your own by using more or less of an ingredient. Also, use different kinds of peppers or chilies.

2 tablespoons chili powder
1/2 teaspoon garlic powder
1/2 teaspoon onion powder
1/2 teaspoon dried oregano
1 teaspoon paprika

1 tablespoons ground cumin
1 teaspoon salt
1 teaspoon black pepper
1 teaspoon crushed red pepper flakes

Mix all ingredients together well. Store in airtight container.

Use this spice blend in ground beef to use for tacos, tostadas or enchiladas. Great flavor for most meats. Add it to scrambled eggs with a dollop of sour cream!

Tandoori Spice - *India*

1 teaspoon ground ginger
1 teaspoon ground cumin
1 teaspoon ground coriander
1 teaspoon paprika
1 teaspoon turmeric

1 teaspoon salt
1 teaspoon cayenne pepper
1 teaspoon garlic powder
1 teaspoon ground nutmeg
1/2 teaspoon dried mint

Mix all ingredients together well. Store in airtight container.

This mix is for that classic Tandoori chicken flavor. You can try it on other meats and veggies too.

* See Indian Tandoori Chicken recipe in the *Recipes* section in this book.

Tomato & Herb Dip Mix - *America*

4 tablespoons tomato powder
1 tablespoon dried onion
2 teaspoons dried parsley
2 teaspoons basil
2 teaspoons oregano

1 teaspoons onion powder
1 teaspoon garlic powder
½ teaspoon dried lemon peel
¼ teaspoon pepper

Mix all ingredients together well. Store in airtight container.

To use:

Mix 2 tablespoons dip mix with 2 cups sour cream or 1 cup sour cream and 1 cup mayonnaise. Stir until well blended. Cover and refrigerate for at least 2 hours before serving. Serve with chips, crackers or veggies.

Tzatziki Dip Mix - Greece

¼ cup dehydrated cucumber
2 tablespoons garlic powder
1 ½ tablespoons dill

1 tablespoon dried lemon peel
1 tablespoon dried mint
¼ teaspoon salt

Mix all ingredients into plastic bag and crush with rolling pin. Store in airtight container.

To serve:

Mix 2 tablespoons dip mix with 2 cups plain Greek yogurt and 1 tablespoon olive oil. Stir until well blended. Cover and refrigerate for at least 2 hours before serving. Serve with chips, crackers, veggies or pita bread triangles.

Vindaloo - *India*

2 teaspoons cumin
1 teaspoon black pepper
1/4 tsp ground cardamom
2 teaspoons cinnamon
2 teaspoons dried mustard
1 teaspoon fenugreek
1 teaspoon black pepper

1/2 teaspoon cloves
2 teaspoons coriander
2 teaspoons fennel
1 teaspoon chili flakes
1 teaspoon garlic powder
1 teaspoon ginger

Mix all ingredients together well. Store in airtight container.

To make paste, mix with 3 tablespoons olive oil and 2 tablespoons vinegar.

* See Vindaloo recipe in the *Recipes* section in this book.

Wasabi Dip Mix - *Japan*

3 tablespoons wasabi powder
2 tablespoons ground sesame
seeds
1 tablespoon garlic powder

1 tablespoon onion flakes
1 teaspoon salt
1 teaspoon ground ginger
½ teaspoon black pepper

Mix all ingredients together well. Store in airtight container.

To use:
Mix 2 tablespoons of mix with 2 cups sour cream and 2 tablespoons soy sauce.
Cover and refrigerate for at least 2 hours before serving. Serve with chips, rice
crackers or veggies.

This dip mix has a unique flavor!

Wasabi Dukkah

2 tablespoons wasabi powder
2 tablespoons blanched almonds
2 tablespoons whole sesame seeds
1 tablespoon garlic powder

1 tablespoon crushed onion flakes
1 teaspoon salt
1 teaspoon ground ginger
½ teaspoon black pepper

Mix all ingredients into plastic bag and crush with rolling pin.   Store in airtight container.

To serve:
Sprinkle over a block of cream cheese and serve with rice crackers or serve with olive oil and bread to dip.

Za'atar Spice Blend - Middle East

1 tablespoon thyme
1 tablespoon oregano
1 tablespoon cumin
1 tablespoon coriander

2 tablespoons sesame seeds, toasted
2 teaspoons ground sumac
½ teaspoon salt

Mix all ingredients together well. Store in airtight container.

A great flavoring for veggies, bread and meat. Or mix with olive oil and drizzle over crusty bread. Add lemon juice and olive oil to the Za'atar and whisk together for a delicious salad dressing. Mix into hummus.

Recipes to Use With Your Spice Blends

Don't limit yourself to these recipes. Experiment with your spice blends to create new and delicious meals.

Filipino Chicken Adobo

Ingredients -

4 to 5 pounds chicken thighs
1/2 cup white vinegar
1/2 cup soy sauce
2 tablespoons Adobo spice blend

To Cook -

Combine all ingredients a large pot. Cover and marinate the chicken in the refrigerator for 1 to 3 hours.

Bring the chicken to a boil over high heat. Lower the heat, cover and let simmer for 30 minutes, stirring occasionally. Remove the lid and simmer until the sauce is reduced and thickened and the chicken is tender, about 20 more minutes.

Serve with steamed rice.

Bahraini Chicken & Rice

Ingredients -

2 large onions, diced

3 tablespoons unsalted butter

2 tablespoons Biryani spice blend

2 tablespoons vegetable oil

3 pounds chicken pieces

1 hot chili pepper (e.g., jalapeno), seeded and diced

1 tablespoon fresh ginger, minced

1 (14 oz) can diced tomatoes, juices drained)

2-3 dried limes (loomi), several holes punched into each one

5 green cardamom pods

2½ teaspoons salt

2½ cups chicken stock

2 cups basmati rice (soak for about 15 minutes, then rinse & drain)

3 tablespoons fresh cilantro, chopped

2 tablespoons fresh parsley, chopped

Rosewater

To Cook -

Heat the oil in a large Dutch oven over medium-high heat and fry the chicken pieces on both sides until the skin is brown and crispy. Transfer the chicken to a plate and leave the remaining oil in the Dutch oven.

Add the butter, reduce the heat to medium, and fry the onions until starting to brown, about 10 to 12 minutes.

Add the ginger and chili pepper and sauté for another 2 minutes. Add the Biryani spice blend and cook for another minute.

Return the chicken pieces to the Dutch oven along with the tomatoes, dried limes, cardamom pods and salt. Add the chicken stock and stir to combine. Bring it to a boil, reduce the heat to low, cover and simmer for one hour.

Add the cilantro, parsley and drained rice and stir to combine. Return it to a boil, reduce the heat to low, cover, and simmer for another 15 to 20 minutes until the rice is done and has absorbed the liquid.

Transfer the chicken and rice to a serving dish and sprinkle with 1 to 2 tablespoons of rosewater (optional).

Tikka Masala

Ingredients -

1 1/2 pounds boneless skinless chicken breasts, thighs, or a mix
1 1/2 cups plain whole milk yogurt
1/4 cup tomato paste
1 28-oz. can crushed tomatoes
4 tablespoons vegetable oil
2 tablespoons Garam Masala spice blend
1 tablespoon crushed garlic

1 tablespoon kosher salt
3 teaspoons peeled ginger, grated
3 teaspoons ground turmeric
1 teaspoon red pepper flakes (optional)
1 small onion, thinly sliced
2 cups heavy cream
Chopped cilantro

To Cook -

Cut chicken into chunks. Combine Garam Masala, garlic, ginger, salt and turmeric in a small bowl. Whisk half of this mixture into the yogurt. Add chicken and turn to coat. Cover and chill for at least 5 hours. Refrigerate remaining spice mixture.

Heat 3 tablespoons oil in a large heavy pot over medium heat. Add onion, tomato paste, and pepper flakes and cook, stirring often, for about 5 minutes. Add remaining half of spice mixture and cook, stirring often, until bottom of pot begins to brown, about 4 more minutes.

Add tomatoes with juices and bring to a boil. Reduce heat and simmer, stirring often and scraping up browned bits from bottom of pot, until sauce thickens, about 10 minutes.

Add cream and chopped cilantro. Simmer, stirring occasionally, until sauce thickens, 30-40 minutes.

Meanwhile, heat 1 tablespoon of oil in a large skillet over medium-high heat. Add the chicken pieces and cook until they're cooked through - about 6 to 7 minutes. Add chicken to sauce mix and stir.

Serve over rice.

Berbere

Sauté minced garlic and thinly sliced ginger in oil until softened. Add a small diced onion and sauté until golden. Mix in a tablespoon of Berbere spice and toss to coat the onions. Add 1 ½ cups of beans (your choice) and 2 diced tomatoes and cook until the tomatoes are soft. Wilt in a bunch of chopped greens or spinach, by the handful, stirring often. Serve over quinoa with a dollop of yogurt, if desired.

Greek Avgolemono Soup

Ingredients -

4 cups chicken stock
1 cup water, divided
1/2 cup orzo
3 teaspoons Greek spice mix

3 egg yolks
1 tablespoon cornstarch
1 cup cooked shredded chicken
2 tablespoons lemon juice

To Cook -

Bring chicken stock, 3/4 cup of the water, orzo and Greek seasoning to boil in 4-quart saucepan. Reduce heat to low; cover and simmer 10 minutes or until orzo is just tender.

Beat egg yolks, remaining 1/4 cup water and cornstarch in large bowl with wire whisk. Gradually whisk in about 2 cups of the hot broth mixture. Slowly whisk egg mixture back into the remaining broth mixture in pan.

Cook on medium-low heat 5 to 7 minutes to slightly thicken. Do not boil. Stir in chicken and lemon juice; cook until heated through. Garnish each serving with thin slice of lemon and chopped parsley, if desired.

Marrakesh Vegetable Curry

Ingredients -

1 zucchini, sliced
1 medium eggplant, cubed
1 sweet potato, peeled and cubed
1 green bell pepper, chopped
1 red bell pepper, chopped
2 carrots, chopped
1 onion, chopped
10 ounces, spinach
6 tablespoons olive oil
1 (15 ounce) can garbanzo beans, drained
1/4 cup blanched almonds
1/4 cup raisins
2 tablespoons Marrakesh Moroccan Spice Blend
1 cup orange juice

To Cook -

In a medium saucepan place olive oil, spice mix and orange juice. Sauté over medium heat for 3 minutes.

Place all veggies in slow cooker except spinach. Pour in heated sauce. Cook on low for 6 hours. Add beans, almonds, raisins and spinach and cook for another 30 minutes.

Peri Peri Chicken

Make a sauce from 2 to 4 tablespoons Peri Peri spice blend and ½ to 1 cup lemon juice. In a large bowl, add chicken to the mixture and rub into meat. Marinate for 3 hours.

Preheat a grill to medium heat. Place chicken onto the grill and discard the marinade. Cook for about 30 minutes, turning occasionally, until the skin is slightly charred and juices run clear.

Moroccan Chicken and Onion Tagine

Ingredients -

Chicken pieces
2 large onions, sliced
3 cloves chopped garlic
1 tablespoon Ras el Hanout spice blend

1/4 to olive oil
1/2 cup water
1/2 cup olives
1 lemon (cut into quarters)
Parsley or cilantro (optional)

To Cook -

This dish is best prepared in a "tagine". Of course, if you don't have one you could use a clay or ceramic baking dish or a Dutch oven. If nothing else, use a deep skillet with a lid.

Place half of the onion slices and the garlic in the bottom of your cooking vessel. Arrange the chicken pieces, skin-side up, on top of the onions.

Sprinkle the spice over the chicken. Add the olive oil, allowing some of it to drizzle over the chicken, and then add the water around the chicken. Arrange the remaining onion rings on top of the chicken.

Cover and place over medium-low heat. Let it heat slowly to a simmer, and then reduce the heat to the lowest temperature possible to maintain the simmer.

Cook for up to two hours - until tender. Test by seeing if you can easily pinch the meat off the bone.

Towards the end of cooking, add the lemon wedges and olives. Make sure there is enough liquid to prevent the onions from scorching. Add a tiny bit of water if necessary - keep in mind that there should be little sauce in the finished tagine.

Garnish with fresh parsley or cilantro and add Moroccan bread to scoop everything up with.

Sri Lankan Coconut Chicken

Ingredients -

4 boneless skinless chicken breasts
1 can coconut milk or cream

2 tablespoons Coconut Spice Blend
2 tablespoons olive oil

To Cook -

Cut chicken breasts in half lengthwise. Roll in Coconut Spice Blend. Fry on medium heat for about 10 minutes, turning as needed, until done. Drain oil from pan and add coconut milk or cream. Simmer on low for about 10 minutes.

Alternative recipes -

You can also grill the chicken on the bar-b-q and omit the coconut milk.

instead of frying the chicken - place chicken, spice blend and coconut milk in slow cooker (omit oil). Cook on high for 4 to 5 hours.

Add in some curry powder to make a delicious chicken coconut curry.

Caribbean Jerk Chicken

Ingredients -

3 tablespoons Jerk spice blend
3 tablespoons vegetable oil
2 tablespoons soy sauce

1 tablespoon cider vinegar
3 pounds bone-in chicken parts

To Cook -

Mix jerk spice blend, oil, soy sauce and vinegar in a large re-sealable plastic bag and mix well. Place chicken in the bag and coat well.

Refrigerate for at least one hour. Remove chicken from marinade and discard remaining marinade.

Grill over medium heat with lid closed 30 to 40 minutes or until chicken is cooked through, turning occasionally.

Indian Tandoori Chicken

Ingredients -

2 pounds boneless skinless chicken, cut into pieces
1 teaspoon salt
1 lemon, juiced
1 1/4 cups plain yogurt
1/2 onion, finely chopped
1 clove garlic, minced
1 teaspoon grated fresh ginger root
2 teaspoons Garam Masala spice blend
1 teaspoon cayenne pepper
2 teaspoons finely chopped cilantro
1 lemon, cut into wedges
1 teaspoon yellow food coloring (optional)
1 teaspoon red food coloring (optional)

To Cook -

Place chicken in a shallow dish. Sprinkle both sides of chicken with salt and lemon juice. Set aside 20 minutes.

In a medium bowl, combine yogurt, onion, garlic, ginger, Garam Masala, and cayenne pepper. Mix until smooth. The food coloring is to make it look authentic, so if you want, stir in yellow and red food coloring. Spread the yogurt mixture over the chicken. Cover, and refrigerate for at least 6 hours (up to 24 hours).

Preheat an outdoor grill for medium high heat, and lightly oil the grate.

Cook the chicken on grill until no longer pink and juices run clear. Garnish with cilantro and lemon wedges.

Slow Cooker Butter Chicken

Ingredients -

2 pounds boneless skinless chicken thighs
2 8-ounce cans tomato paste
1 8-ounce can tomato sauce
1 15-ounce can coconut milk
1 tablespoon minced ginger
3 teaspoons minced garlic
1/2 onion, finely diced

2 teaspoons Garam Masala
1 teaspoon curry powder
1/2 teaspoon cinnamon
1 teaspoon salt
1 teaspoon pepper
3 tablespoons butter ½ cup plain Greek yogurt
More butter

Directions -

Cut chicken into bite-size pieces. Mince the onion (I actually grate it so it's very fine).

Put all ingredients except chicken into freezer bag or bowl and mix well. Add chicken and mix again.

To Cook -

Place mixture in slow cooker. Cook 8 hours on low.

Right before serving, stir in yogurt and another tablespoon or two of butter.

Serve with: cooked brown rice and green veggies

Beef or Chicken Vindaloo

Ingredients -

2 pounds boneless skinless chicken thighs cut into chunks or beef chunks
2 8-ounce cans tomato paste
1 8-ounce can tomato sauce
1 15-ounce can coconut milk
2 cups onion, finely diced
1 tablespoon olive oil
1 to 2 tablespoons Vindaloo spice blend

To Cook -

Brown meat in oil with onions. Add all other ingredients. Bring to a boil over high heat, then reduce heat to medium-low, cover, and simmer until the about 20 minutes. Remove the cover, and cook 5 minutes more to thicken slightly.

Serve over rice with a dollop of plain Greek yogurt if you wish.

Spice Substitutions

Allspice – Cinnamon, cassia, dash of nutmeg or mace, or a dash of cloves

Anise – Fennel seed or a few drops anise extract

Basil – Oregano or thyme

Bay leaf – Thyme, basil or oregano

Black pepper – White pepper, paprika

Caraway – Celery seed

Cardamom – Ginger

Celery – Caraway or dill (use less)

Chervil – Tarragon or parsley

Cilantro – Parsley

Cinnamon – Nutmeg or allspice (use only 1/4 of the amount)

Coriander – Cumin or tarragon

Cloves – Allspice, cinnamon, or nutmeg

Cumin – Caraway, chili powder or coriander.

Dill – Fennel or basil

Fennel – Anise, dill or caraway

Garlic – Onion

Ginger – Allspice, cinnamon, mace, or nutmeg

Italian Seasoning – Blend of any of these: basil, oregano, rosemary, and ground red pepper

Mace – Allspice with a pinch of nutmeg, cinnamon or ginger

Marjoram – Basil, thyme, or savory

Mint – Basil, marjoram, or rosemary

Mustard – Turmeric

Nettle – Spinach powder or dried spinach flakes

Nutmeg – Cinnamon, ginger, or mace

Onion – Onion flakes, garlic powder or dried chives

Oregano – Thyme or basil

Paprika – Half the amount of cayenne powder or black pepper. If using for color, you can also use chili or chipotle powder

Parsley – Chervil or cilantro

Poultry Seasoning – Sage plus a blend of any of these: thyme, marjoram, savory, black pepper, and rosemary

Rosemary – Thyme, tarragon, or savory

Saffron – Dash turmeric (for color)

Sage – Poultry seasoning, savory, marjoram, or rosemary

Savory – Thyme, marjoram, or sage

Sumac – Lemon zest, amchoor

Tarragon – Chervil, dash fennel seed, or dash aniseed

Thyme – Basil, marjoram, oregano, or savory

Turmeric – Curry powder, cumin, ginger

White Pepper – Black pepper

Which Spice for Which Food?

Don't limit yourself to this list. Experiment with your spices, herbs and blends to come up with new recipes.

Basil is good on or in tomatoes, tomato sauces, peas, squash, lamb, fish, eggs, tossed salad, cheese, potatoes, pasta.

Bay leaf is good on or in vegetable and fish soups, tomato sauces, poached fish and meat stews.

Cinnamon is good in or on baked goods, sauces, savory meat dishes and fruits. Add a little cinnamon to meat dishes for a new taste.

Cumin is good in savory recipes, like chili, stews, meat, fish, and vegetables. Used quite often in Middle Eastern dishes.

Dill is good on or in fish, cream and cottage cheese, potatoes, fish, vegetable salads, pickles, tomatoes

Marjoram is good on or in fish, vegetable soups, cheese dishes, stew, roast chicken, beef, pork, stuffing

Mint is good on or in jellies, fruit juices, candies, frosting, cakes, pies, pork, potatoes, peas and chocolate

Nutmeg is good in or on sweet potatoes, red potatoes, carrots, pumpkin, winter squash, cabbage, broccoli, cauliflower, spinach and in milk or egg based foods like eggnog or puddings.

Oregano is good on or in tomato sauces, pork, pizza, vegetable and fish salads, and chili.

Parsley is good on or in meats, vegetables, soups, eggs, cheese

Rosemary is good on or in poultry stuffing, potatoes, cauliflower, fish

Sage is good on or in stuffing, pork roast, sausage, poultry and hamburgers

Savory is good on or in eggs, meats, salads, chicken, soups and stuffing

Tarragon is good on or in fish sauces, egg and cheese dishes, green salads, pickles, chicken, tomatoes, carrots, sauces for meats and vegetables

Thyme is good on or in soups, stuffing, beef, pork dishes, eggs, cheese, bean and vegetable soups and fish

Turmeric is good in soups, rice dishes and veggies.

~*~*~*~*~*~

What Foods Call for Which Spice or Herb

Beef: Bay leaf, basil, cayenne, celery, chili, coriander, garlic, curry, dill, ginger, mustard, paprika, marjoram, oregano, parsley, rosemary, sage, thyme.

Beets: Allspice, nutmeg.

Bread: Cinnamon, coconut flour, dill, garlic, Italian spices, powdered cheese, rosemary.

Broccoli: Mustard, nutmeg, sage.

Carrots: Dill, nutmeg, parsley, rosemary, tarragon, thyme.

Chicken: garlic, marjoram, tarragon, oregano, coriander.

Cucumbers: Basil, dill, lemon pepper, mint, parsley.

Eggplant: Oregano, parsley.

Eggs: Chili powder, garlic, turmeric.

Fish (fried): mustard, oregano, tarragon, sage.

Fish (grilled): coriander, dill, fennel, ginger, parsley, rosemary, thyme.

Fruit: Allspice, anise, cinnamon, cloves, curry, ginger, mace, mint, nutmeg, pepper.

Green Beans: Dill, marjoram, nutmeg, oregano.

Ground Beef: Garlic powder, onion powder, red pepper flakes, rosemary.

Ham: Cloves, mustard powder, tarragon.

Lamb: Basil, cardamom, cinnamon, curry, dill, garlic, mace, marjoram, mint, oregano, paprika, parsley, rosemary, turmeric.

Mushrooms: Garlic, sage.

Peas: Marjoram, mint.

Pork: Allspice, basil, cardamom, cloves, curry, garlic, ginger, marjoram, mustard, oregano, paprika, parsley, rosemary, sage, savory, thyme.

Potatoes: Chives, cumin, dill, fennel, garlic, mace, rosemary, tarragon.

Rice: Chives, cumin, curry, nutmeg, parsley, saffron, turmeric.

Squash: Cardamom, basil, garlic, ginger, nutmeg.

Tomato : Allspice, basil, cloves, cumin, dill, fennel, marjoram, oregano.

Turkey: Allspice, anise, basil, bay leaf, cayenne, cumin, curry, dill, ginger, marjoram, mustard, nutmeg, oregano, paprika, parsley, pepper, rosemary, sage, savory, tarragon, thyme.

Medicinal Uses for Spices & Herbs

Cayenne -

Helps with arthritis and muscle pain

Aids in shingles pain and diabetes-related nerve pain

Anti-inflammatory and antioxidant

Cold remedy, since cayenne shrinks blood vessels in your nose and throat, relieving congestion

Metabolism booster

May have anti-diabetes benefits

Cinnamon -

Improves blood sugar control

Cuts cholesterol levels

Can help prevent blood clots

High in fiber

Can reduce heartburn

Cloves -

Has anti-inflammatory effects

Rank high in antioxidant properties

Slows cartilage and bone damage caused by arthritis

Has a numbing effect in addition to bacteria-fighting powers

Coriander (actually cilantro seeds) -

Acts as a digestive aid

Helps with irritable bowel syndrome, as it calms intestinal spasms that can lead to diarrhea

Relieves antianxiety

Has been shown to lower cholesterol in animals.

Cumin -

Aids with bloating

Used to start menstruation

Said to increase sexual desire

Garlic -

When eaten daily, garlic can help lower heart disease risk by as much as 76 percent

It moderately reduces cholesterol levels

Garlic thins the blood

It appears to ward off cancer, especially stomach and colorectal cancer

Garlic can help with yeast infections, some sinus infections, and the common cold

It repels ticks and mosquitos

Ginger -

Can be used as a digestive aid

Combats inflammation

Reduces pain and swelling in people with arthritis

It may work against migraines

Proven to be effective against nausea

Mace -

Can reduce flatulence

Aids digestion

Improve the appetite

Treats diarrhea, vomiting and nausea.

Mustard -

Studies suggest it may inhibit the growth of cancer cells

Breaks up congestion

Stimulate appetite by increasing the flow of saliva and digestive juices

Mustard powder added to a footbath helps kill athlete's foot fungus

Don't consume too much because it can have a laxative effect or induce vomiting

Sage -

Is a known as a memory enhancer

Improves mood

Increases alertness and/or calmness

It appears to boost the action of insulin and reduce blood sugar

Health Benefits of Turmeric

Promotes a Balanced Mood. Turmeric has long been used in Chinese medicine as a treatment for depression.

Aches and Discomfort relief

Encourages Balanced Blood Sugar

Soothes Irritated Tissue

Helps Stiff Joints

Regulates Cholesterol Levels

May aid in fat metabolism and help in **weight management.**

Indigestion and heartburn aid

Cancer - Doctors at UCLA found that turmeric appeared to block an enzyme that promotes the growth of head and neck cancer.

Powerful antioxidant

Helps Wounds Heal

Potent anti-inflammatory

Relieves Arthritis

Helps Prevent Heart Disease - Studies have suggested curcumin may help prevent the buildup of plaque that can clog arteries and lead to heart attacks and strokes.

Brain Protection - In a recent study, researchers found turmeric promotes repair to stems cells in the brain.

When combined with cauliflower, turmeric has shown to **prevent prostate cancer** and stop the growth of existing prostate cancer.

Turmeric may **prevent and slow the progression of Alzheimer's disease** by removing amyloid plaque buildup in the brain.

Turmeric Cautions

Gallbladder problems: Turmeric can make gallbladder problems worse. Do not use turmeric if you have gallstones or a bile duct obstruction.

Iron deficiency: Taking high amounts of turmeric might prevent the absorption of iron. Turmeric should be used with caution in people with iron deficiency.

Do not use in large amounts when pregnant.

Infertility: Turmeric might lower testosterone levels and decrease sperm movement when taken by mouth by men. This might reduce fertility. Turmeric should be used cautiously by people trying to have a baby.

Take Turmeric Cautiously With These Medications

Turmeric may neutralize the effect of **Antacids** like -

· Cimetidine (Tagamet)

· Famotidine (Pepcid)

· Ranitidine (Zantac)

· Omeprazole

Because turmeric thins the blood, use it sparingly if you are on **Blood Thinners** like -

· Aspirin

· Clopidogrel (Plavix)

· Dipyridamole (Persantine)

· Ticlopidine (Ticlid)

· Warfarin (Coumadin, Jantoen)

· Enoxaparin (Lovenox)

Turmeric can lower blood sugar so if you are taking **Diabetes Meds** keep a check on your blood sugar.

· Sulfonylureas

· Biguanides

· Meglitinides

· Thiazolidinediones

· DPP-4 inhibitors

· SGLT2 inhibitors

· Alpha-glucosidase inhibitors

· Bile acid sequestrants

ABOUT THE AUTHOR

Ann has always liked ethnic foods. When traveling, she always tries the local cuisine.

In 2010, Ann started doing freezer meal workshops to help people save time and money. Soon after starting the freezer workshops, she started doing Spice Blending workshops.

She not only does the workshops for people who want to host in their homes but also for five different city's recreation programs and private corporations.

Ann is the author of several books, including books about freezer meal workshops, direct marketing business and the childcare business.

Check them out at www.annieshousepublishing.com

Made in the USA
Middletown, DE
25 August 2022

71422524R00040